J O H N   C O U

LIVING THE ...

Sikh Lives

O L I V E R & B O Y D

Acknowledgements

The author would like to thank all those who have helped him to write this book, and given permission for family photographs to be used. Thanks are also due to Mr Sucha Singh Gill, J.P., for reading the script and giving helpful advice.

The publishers thank the following for permission to reproduce photographs on the pages listed:
Cover: Sikh bride, David Richardson; Temple leaders, Select/David Harden; Temple, ZEFA Picture Library; pp. 5, 9: Ann & Bury Peerless Slide Resources and Picture Library; pp. 10, 12: North Kent Weekly News; p. 16: Peerless; pp. 18, 20: North Kent Weekly News; pp. 22, 23, 25, 26, 29: John Coutts; p. 30: Kentish Times; pp. 31, 32: John Coutts; pp. 36, 37, 39: Select/David Harden; pp. 41, 43, 44, 45: Phil Weedon.

Oliver & Boyd
Longman House
Burnt Mill
Harlow, Essex,
CM20 2JE, England
and Associated Companies throughout the world
An imprint of Longman Group UK Ltd

ISBN 0 05 004512 1
First published 1990

Typeset on Apple Macintosh SE/30 in Palatino 11/15pt by Word Power, Edinburgh.
Produced by Longman Group (F.E.) Ltd
Printed in Hong Kong

CONTENTS

THE TEN GURUS

Guru Nanak was the first of the ten **Gurus**, each of whom has contributed to the Sikh religion as practised today.

ANGAD (second Guru) 1539-1552CE
* wrote down Nanak's hymns in the Gurmukhi script.

'IK OANKAR' ('There is one God') in Gurmukhi writing.
Look out for this if you visit a Sikh temple.

AMAR DAS (third Guru) 1552-1574
* forbade the custom of burning widows alive when the bodies of their husbands were cremated. This custom was called **sati**.
* persuaded the Emperor Akbar to share a meal in the communal dining hall (**langar**).
* composed the **Anand Sahib** (Hymn of Bliss).
'Listen to me...my fortunate friends.
I have reached God, the supreme spirit,
and all my sorrows have vanished...'
(from the Hymn of Bliss)
This is sung near the end of a service (in Britain this is usually held on Sunday mornings).

RAM DAS (fourth Guru) 1574-1581
* constructed a large tank called Amrit Sar ('The pool of nectar'). Round the pool grew up the city of Amritsar.
* composed the four verses (**lavan**) which are sung at the most holy part of a Sikh wedding. As they are sung, bride and groom become one.

The Ten Gurus. Guru Nanak is in the centre. The two figures without haloes are attendants not Gurus.

ARJAN (fifth Guru) 1581-1606
  * began to build the **Harimandir** (Golden Temple) in Amritsar.
  * compiled the Sikh Scriptures (the **Guru Granth Sahib**) and placed a copy in the Golden Temple.
  * was tortured to death by the Mogul Emperor Jehangir, who was hostile to the Sikhs.
HARGOBIND (sixth Guru) 1606-1644
  * began to organise Sikh resistance.
  * provided his troops with a pennant which became the yellow flag of Sikhism (the **nishan sahib**).
  * worked out the theory of the two swords, standing for political power and spiritual power.

* built the **Akal Takht** ('Eternal Throne') next to the Golden Temple. There he sat on a throne higher than that of the Emperor!

HAR RAI (seventh Guru) 1644-1661

* refused to see his son ever again, because he had failed to stand up for the faith before the Emperor.

HAR KRISHNAN (eighth Guru) 1661-1664)

* became Guru at the age of five. He died of smallpox.

TEGH BAHADUR (ninth Guru) 1664-1675

* forgave the man who tried to shoot him. He said, 'To forgive is equal to bathing in all places of pilgrimage'.
* protested to the Emperor Aurungzeb who was trying to impose Islam by force. He refused to become a Muslim and was beheaded for his faith.

GOBIND SINGH (tenth Guru) 1675-1708

* organised the Sikh brotherhood (**Khalsa**) and gave them the 'Five Ks' (see page 00) as signs of their faith.
* declared that there would be no more human Teachers (**Gurus**). In future the Scriptures (**Guru Granth Sahib**) would be the guide for the Sikh community.

The khanda symbol shows two swords, which stand for political and spiritual power

INTRODUCTION

*T*his book is about the Sikh religion. It tells stories about the Teachers who founded the Sikh faith centuries ago, in India, and also takes us to meet people who live by that faith today.

THE FAITH OF THE TEN GURUS

The first section gives the history of the Sikh religion from the time when it was founded by Guru Nanak in the fifteenth century. We find out about Nanak's attempt to combine what was best in the Hindu and Muslim religions, and we learn the basic points of his teaching about how to find God.

RITUAL, CEREMONY AND FESTIVAL

The second section introduces us to the Sikh religion in practice. We meet some musicians and find out about the music and song which is an important part of their faith. Next we learn about the Festival of Baisakhi, as it is celebrated in an English town. On this day, in 1699, the Sikh nation was born and the ceremony of baptism introduced. We meet a young British Sikh and discover what baptism means for her. Then we are invited to a wedding and learn the meaning of the solemn and simple ceremony which joins man and woman in the presence of God.

CARING, SHARING AND HEALING

The third section shows us the Sikh faith in action. We hear the story of Puran Singh, who has dedicated his life to the care of disabled people in India, and we find out about the faith of Jastinder, who prayed for the life of her son after he was injured in an accident in a London street.

Important people, writings or events in the faith of Sikhism are referred to as follows:

Section 1: Guru Nanak, Mool Mantra, Sanghat, Gurdwara, Langar, Ten Gurus, Khalistan.

Section 2: Amrit Kirtan, Raga, Guru Granth Sahib, Baisakhi, Khanda, Khalsa, 'Five Ks', Amrit, Singh/Kaur (names), Five Beloved, Waheguru, Granthi, Wedding Hymn (Lavan), Gutka, Romalla, Karah Parshad.

Section 3: Divali, Pingal/Pingalwara, Japji, Sat Nam, Akand Path.

Pupil activities are suggested at the end of each chapter. A word list, giving explanations of Sikh terms or words which need comment, is provided at the end of the book. Words included in the list are printed in **bold type** in the text.

Guru Nanak

Historical Background

*T*he word 'Sikh' means 'disciple': Sikhs are followers of a number of Teachers or gu**rus** who have taught about God. The essential Sikh message is found in the Holy Book, the **Guru Granth Sahib**.

The Sikh faith began in the Punjab in north-western India. The ancient religion of India – Hinduism – includes the worship of many gods and goddesses. These can be represented, through pictures or statues, in human or animal form. Such belief in many gods is called **polytheism**.

Into India from the north-west came **Islam**, the faith taught by the prophet Muhammad. Muhammad declared that there was only One God, and that God was far too great to be represented in human form. To the followers of Islam, which means 'believers in One God only' the many images and statues of the Hindus were idols. Belief in one God only is called **monotheism**.

Sometimes there was friendship between Hindus and Muslims – but there was also misunderstanding and conflict. Much of northern India was ruled from Delhi by a Muslim, the Mogul Emperor, and sometimes the Emperor tried to impose the faith of Islam by force.

GURU NANAK

This was the world into which Nanak, the founder of the Sikh faith, was born. His family, which followed the Hindu faith, lived in the village of Talwandi where Nanak was born in the year 1469 CE. As

Nanak grew up the strife between the two religions worried him. He thought that neither the Hindus nor the Muslims had found the complete truth. It made Nanak very sad that people should fight each other for their faith. He himself looked for truth in both religions.

Many stories are told about Nanak's prayers, his life of love, and his search for God. One day, it is said, he went to bathe in the river and did not come back. Friends and family searched for him in vain. They dragged the river for his body but without success. Sadly, they decided that he had been drowned.

But three days later Nanak came back. He had been, he said, at the court of God himself. There he had been given a cup of nectar (a sweet drink).

"I was a minstrel out of work", declared Nanak, "The Lord gave me employment. The Mightly One instructed me: 'Night and day sing my praise'."

Nanak had been given a new message about God and he decided to pass it on. First he changed the way he dressed. He looked odd, for he wore the loincloth of a Hindu, together with the headdress of a Muslim preacher. This was meant to drive home the message, 'There

Inside a Sikh temple in England. There is a picture of Guru Nanak above the shrine where the Holy Book is kept

is neither Muslim nor Hindu', and to unite both religions in the worship of the One God.

Nanak set out to spread his message far and wide. He took with him a Hindu peasant, Bala, and a Muslim musician named Mardana, who helped to put the message into song. They travelled through India and beyond. Nanak's followers were the first Sikhs.

NANAK AND HINDUISM

Nanak shared many Hindu beliefs. Like the Hindus, he believed in a spiritual world. Many people wrongly thought that money, power, food or sex were all that mattered. They were trapped in a world of illusion (**maya**) where thay could not find God. Nanak wanted to help them to escape.

Nanak also shared the Hindu belief that after a person died, the soul would return to earth in another body. Depending on that person's deeds in the previous life, they might be a human or an animal. It might take unthinkable ages for them to escape from the round of rebirths and return to the God who made them. This belief in return and rebirth is called **reincarnation**.

However, Nanak also rejected many Hindu ideas. First of all, he said, there was only One God. Any image of Him would be an idol.

Hinduism also maintained the **caste** system, by which people were divided from birth into fixed groups. The four main castes were: Priests, Warriors, Traders and Farmers. Outside the system were the 'Untouchables'. Nanak condemned the caste system. All men and women, he declared, were equal before God. He himself came from the Warrior caste and yet he was teaching about God – a task which had been reserved for Priests.

Many Hindus also chose to suffer extreme forms of hardship, or **asceticism.** Some lived alone in the forest, as hermits, hoping that fasting would bring help to find God. Wrong, said Nanak! It was much better to live in families and help your neighbours in a practical way. You should live in the world without allowing the world to affect you. After all, a duck can swim without getting its feathers wet! Nanak wrote:

> 'The lotus in the water is not wet,
> Nor the waterfowl in the stream.
> If man would live, but by the world untouched,
> Meditate and repeat the name of the Lord supreme.'

The Mool Mantra

Nanak expressed his faith in a hymn that now forms part of the Sikh morning prayer. This is the **Mool Mantra** or 'root belief'.

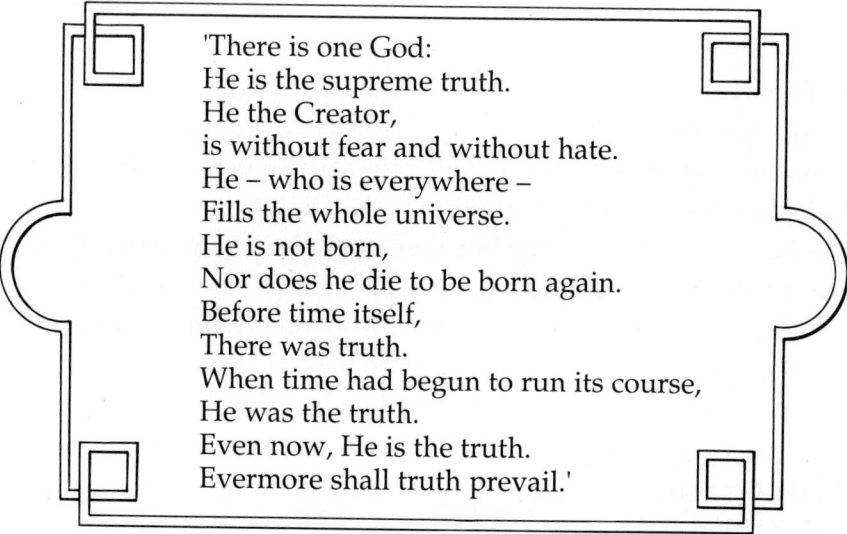

> 'There is one God:
> He is the supreme truth.
> He the Creator,
> is without fear and without hate.
> He – who is everywhere –
> Fills the whole universe.
> He is not born,
> Nor does he die to be born again.
> Before time itself,
> There was truth.
> When time had begun to run its course,
> He was the truth.
> Even now, He is the truth.
> Evermore shall truth prevail.'

THE SIKH COMMUNITY

Nanak taught his followers to work hard, to help the poor and to find God through prayer.

> 'When sin soils the soul action alone shall make it whole.
> Words do not the saint or sinner make.
> Action alone is written in the book of fate.'

He spent the last years of his life at the village of Kartaspur, where the Sikh community (**sanghat**) gathered around him. Here the first temple (**gurdwara**) was built, with its communal dining-hall (**langar**). Eating together was intended to break down the barriers of sex and caste.

Nanak taught through action as well as word. It is said that when he saw some Hindus throwing water towards the sun, as an offering to their ancestors, Nanak threw water in the opposite direction. If you can send water up to heaven, he told them, then surely I can send it back to my fields in the Punjab!

The temple shrine

NANAK AND ISLAM

Nanak agreed with the Muslims that there is only One God, who is far too great and too mysterious to be represented in human form. You will often see pictures of Nanak in a Sikh temple, but they are not idols, and are never to be worshipped. Nanak was very willing to learn from Muslim teachers. He and his followers enjoyed the hymns of Kabir, who wrote:

'If God be within the mosque, to whom does this world belong?
All the men and women of the world are his living forms.'

Over five hundred of Kabir's hymns came to be included in the **Guru Granth Sahib**.

But Nanak also rejected some of the teachings of Islam. He did not agree that Muhammad was the last of God's prophets; he did not see why women should follow the Muslim custom of veiling their faces; and he rejected the idea that pork was 'unclean' meat, just as he would not treat Untouchables as 'unclean' people.

Muslims face the city of Mecca when performing their prayers. It is said that Nanak once fell asleep with his feet pointing in that direction. A Muslim woke him up and pointed out his mistake.

"Show me," said Nanak, "a place where God is *not*, and I will point my feet in that direction."

THE SIKHS IN THE WIDER WORLD

The Sikhs fought back against the Mogul Emperors. In the early nineteenth century they had a strong kingdom of their own, but British power in India was increasing. After the death of the great Sikh ruler, Ranjit Singh, the land of the Sikhs became part of the British Empire.

Many Sikhs served in the Indian army, taking part in the two world wars. But after the First World War (1914–1918) an Independence movement began. In 1919, at the time of the festival of **Baisakhi** (see page 00), over four hundred people were shot dead in Amritsar on the orders of the British General Dyer. The Sikhs now had new martyrs.

After the Second World War (1939–1945) the end of British rule in India was in sight. But many Muslims would not agree to live in a state which they thought would be controlled by the majority group, the Hindus. They called for **Partition**, the division of the Empire of India. And so, in 1947, two new states came into existence: these were India, where there was a Hindu majority, and the largely Muslim Pakistan.

The Sikhs' homeland was divided. Guru Nanak's birthplace, Talwandi, found itself in Pakistan, as did Lahore, once the capital of Ranjit Singh. But Amritsar, home of the Golden Temple, was in India, along with much of the Sikh population.

The Partition of India. In 1947 the Empire of India was divided into two states, India and Pakistan

Terrible times followed. Long lines of refugees trekked past each other. Muslims moved west towards Pakistan while Sikhs and Hindus struggled eastwards towards India. In the years that followed, many Sikhs sought their fortunes abroad, in Canada, the United States of America, East Africa and Great Britain.

'LAND OF THE PURE'

In the new Republic of India the Sikhs lived for some years in peace and prosperity. They formed the majority in Punjab State, and a Sikh became President of the Republic. So perhaps they still held the power of the Two Swords – spiritual and political rule?

Some people thought partition was not enough. They considered that the Hindus were too powerful in India. They believed that the 'sword of political rule' meant a completely independent country for the Sikhs, which would be called Khalistan, the 'Land of the Pure'.

A young Sikh leader, Sant Bhindranwale, took over the Golden Temple in Amritsar. He defied the Indian Government, which claimed that his men were terrorists. Troops surrounded the Temple, but Bhindranwale went on calling for an independent State of Khalistan. Killings continued. Negotiations failed. On 5 June 1984, the Indian Army launched 'Operation Blue Star' to retake the Temple.

Bhindranwale and his men fought much harder than was expected. The Indian Army tried not to shoot at the Golden Temple itself, but the Eternal Throne (**Akal Takht**), built by Guru Hargobind to represent the power of the Sikhs, was smashed by the fire of heavy tanks. Bhindranwale wa killed, with many other defenders. Many thought – and still think – that he died a martyr, a second Guru Gobind Singh.

'Operation Blue Star' was a terrible blow to Sikhs all round the world. Their holiest temple had been attacked. But Mrs Indira Gandhi, the Indian Prime Minister, declared that she had no wish to

The Golden Temple
at Amritsar

harm the Sikh religion. The Golden Temple was repaired and the Prime Minister continued to entrust her life to Sikh soldiers and policemen. On 31 November 1984, two of them shot her dead as she set off to work. They thought her death would avenge the attack on the Golden Temple.

More terrible killings and counter-killings followed. Some Sikhs do support the idea of an independent state of Khalistan, but the BBC's correspondent in India, Mark Tully, wrote in 1986, 'We believe that most Sikhs want moderation to triumph.'

On 7 January 1989, two men convicted of the killing of Mrs Gandhi were hanged. One of them, Satwant Singh, declared before his death, "I wish to be born over and over again, and each time to be able to die for the protection of the Golden Temple."

'Evermore shall truth prevail', declares the **Mool Mantra**. But how? Are the Sikhs a nation, or a religion, or both? What does it mean to live the life of a Sikh in the late twentieth century?

In the next chapters we shall try to find out.

What do you remember?

Join these sentences correctly:

1. The word SIKH means	a Teacher sent by God.
2. The GURU GRANTH SAHIB is	the holy city of the Sikhs.
3. AMRITSAR is	the Sikh Holy Book.
4. A GURU is	a disciple.

What do you know?

Complete these sentences using the correct words:

5. Guru Nanak agreed with Hindu beliefs about:
   a) the caste system
   b) reincarnation.
   c) living alone as a hermit.

6. Guru Nanak agreed with Muslim beliefs about:
   a) facing Mecca to pray.
   b) not eating pork.
   c) worshipping only one God.
   d) accepting Muhammad as the final prophet.

7. The KHALSA is:
   a) the 'Eternal Throne' in Amritsar.
   b) the Sikh Brotherhood, 'the pure'.
   c) the sword carried by some Sikhs.
   d) the yellow flag of the Sikhs.

8. 'IK OANKAR' means:
   a) 'There is neither Hindu nor Muslim.'
   b) 'Evermore shall truth prevail.'
   c) 'God is one.'
   d) 'Sing the praise of God.'

What do you think?

9. 'Untouchables' were outside the caste system in India. Who are the equivalent of 'untouchables' nowadays? How might they be helped?
10. The Sikhs began with a message of peace but at last they had to fight back. Can non-violence ever succeed?

More things to do

11. Make a poster illustrating the words of the Mool Mantra.
12. Write a play or story about what happened when Nanak arrived in a village with his new message about God and humanity. Show how some people were angry, or amused, or interested, or convinced.
13. Imagine that Guru Nanak has returned and has been given the chance to record his message to the twentieth century in a 'one minute spot' for the radio. Write and record his message to your town or country (about 90-100 words).

Learning Through Music and Song

A Meeting with Sikh Musicians

*T*o find out about the Sikh religion I decided to begin with music. The Sikh faith was born in song five hundred years ago, and it still lives in song.

My music lesson took place at the back of the Marharajah Restaurant in Gillingham, Kent. The owner, Mr Sucha Singh Gill, plays the **tabla**, a pair of drums. To help him he had called in Giani Amarjeet Singh, the Head Priest of the local Sikh Temple (**gurdwara**). Also invited was Gian Singh Surjit, an expert musician and music teacher.

Sikh musicians, Mr Sucha Singh Gill, Mr Giani Amarjeet Singh and Mr Gian Singh Surjit

Gian Singh Surjit is blind. He plays only religious music, for his life is dedicated to God.

The tabla consists of a pair of drums. You play the smaller one with your right hand and the larger one, making deeper notes, with your left hand. Gian Singh Surjit was to play the harmonium, pumping the bellows with the right hand and playing the notes with the left. Giani Amarjeet Singh, who is also an expert on the sitar (the Indian guitar), was going to sing.

We sat crossed-legged on the floor. Mr Sucha Singh Gill carefully unwrapped a thick square book printed in Punjabi writing. This was the **Amrit Kirtan**, a selection of the most popular hymns found in the hymn book of the Sikh religion.

We took off our shoes and covered our heads as a mark of respect for the holy book. Amrit Kirtan means something like 'sweetness of singing'. The Holy Book itself, the Granth, is even more special. Sikhs believe that it contains the most important truths that God has ever made known. It is kept in a room of its own, on a special bed. Sikhs call it 'Noble Teacher'. In the Punjabi language it is called the **Guru Granth Sahib.**

The harmonium began to play. Gian Singh Surjit struck up an Indian melody. Sucha Singh Gill joined in on the drums slowly and quietly at first, and then more loudly and quickly. I had no idea that there were so many different notes in the tabla! Then Giani Amarjeet Singh joined in, and I guessed that he was singing a hymn of praise to God in the Punjabi language. The voice, the harmonium and the drums made sweet patterns of sound. The three musicians smiled. They did not need to look down at the open book: they knew the words by heart and loved them.

No wonder they call it 'sweetness of singing'! Fingers moved faster as the music became more complicated. The drummer closed his eyes. Behind his dark glasses Gian Singh Surjit made the harmonium sound louder and more exciting. But the Punjabi words that Giani Amarjeet Singh sang were still clear and plain.

"This is how it all started," I thought to myself. When Guru Nanak set off on his mission, with Bala and Mardana, he used music to put across his message of peace and love.

And when the singing stopped Sucha Singh Gill told me more of the secrets of Indian music. "People often forget if you just give them a lecture," he told me. "When you turn what you want to say into song – then the audience tries to listen. And then they learn."

I also discovered that there are special tunes called **ragas** to go with the hymns in the Granth. Some tunes are intended for use in the morning and some in the afternoon. By singing them at the right time and in the right way, your soul can 'tune in' to God.

Sucha Singh Gill gave me a translation of the words they had sung:

'O God, You are our Father, and we are your children
And whatever you do for us, we are grateful.
We can only live when You give us protection and keep us
safe...and in that protection we can find peace and comfort.'

So the song was a prayer! My three friends had sung for me about their faith in God – just as the Sikhs have been doing for five centuries.

I was then invited to share a meal in the restaurant. It was an east-west dinner and included pizza topped with Indian herbs and spices. Sharing food is also an important part of the Sikh faith. It is a way of saying that all men and women, no matter what their race or caste, are brothers and sisters before God.

Sharing food is an important part of the Sikh faith

What do you remember?

Join these sentences correctly:

1. A TABLA is   the holy book of the Sikhs.
2. A RAGA is a collection of Sikh hymns.
3. AMRIT KIRTAN is   a pair of drums.
4. The GRANTH is a tune in Indian music.

What do you know?

5. Complete this sentence using the correct words:

Because it is considered a holy book,   a)   written in Punjabi.

the Guru Granth b)   kept on a bed in a special   Sahib is: room.

c)   sung only in the morning.

d)   worshipped instead of God.

What do you think?

6. Do you agree that people learn more easily if they are taught through music and song?

7. 'By singing in the right time and in the right way, your soul can "tune in" to God.' Do you agree with this?

More things to do

8. Find out more about Indian music. Listen to a cassette or watch a video. Say why you like it, or do not like it.

9. Gian Singh Surjit plays only religious music, for his life is dedicated to God. Is there a difference between 'religious' and 'other' music? If so, what is it? Talk or write about this.

JOINING THE FAITH

Baisakhi and Baptism in Gravesend

The Baisakhi procession moves through the streets of Gravesend

*I*t is 13 April. The Sikh temple has been prepared for a day of celebration. Outside, on the tall flagpole, flutters a bright yellow flag bearing the emblem of the faith, the **khanda**.
In front of the temple stands a truck, and on the truck is a splendid model of the Golden Temple in Amritsar. On the front, for all to see, are portraits of Nanak, the first Guru, and Gobind Singh, the tenth Guru.

Behind the model temple a long procession has formed. There are children from the Punjabi School, wearing bright

Children from the Guru Nanak school join the procession

On the day of the procession, a van is decorated with portraits of gurus and of Bhindranwale, the Sikh who died in the attack on the Golden Temple in Amritsar

yellow headscarves. There is the Guru Nanak football club. We can also see the International Sikh Youth Federation, and a car parked in the street bears a poster showing the bearded face of the Sikh Bhindranwale, who died in the attack on the Golden Temple in Amritsar. In some British temples, too, there has been tension – even violence. But today is a festival of peace.

Stewards give out a free pamphlet to explain to bystanders the meaning of Baisakhi. Originally a Harvest Festival, it is also famous as the birthday of the **Khalsa**, the Sikh Brotherhood. People have come from far and wide to celebrate the creation of an army of soldier-saints who would be prepared to sacrifice their lives for the defence of the weak and the oppressed.

THE KHALSA AND THE FIVE KS

On the first day of the month Baisakh (13 April), in 1699, the young Guru Gobind Singh assembled his followers at Anandpur. It was high time to fight back against the attacks of the Mogul Emperor! But who, he asked, was brave enough to die for the faith? There was silence. At last a volunteer came forward. Gobind Singh took him behind a curtain – and reappeared with a sword dripping with blood. He called for a second...third...fourth...fifth volunteer. Each man disappeared in turn – and each, it seemed, had his head cut off.

But then Gobind Singh reappeared – with the five volunteers alive at his side! "These are the Five Beloved Ones," he said. "They have offered their heads to me, and they shall always be filled with my spirit."

Some say that a goat was beheaded behind the screen as each of the Five came forward for the bravery test. But many Sikhs believe that Gobind Singh really did cut off the heads of the Five and restore them to life.

Following this came the first-ever Sikh baptism. The Guru poured water into an iron basin: then his wife added sugar crystals, for women were also to be free to join the Brotherhood. The Guru then stirred the water with a double-edged sword, reciting prayers as he did so. By the power of God, the sweet water became nectar, a**mrit**, giving strength to the disciples.

Each of the five was given five palmsful of nectar to drink from the same vessel. They came from different castes, and drinking from the same vessel symbolised the end of the unjust caste system. Then the nectar was sprinkled five times on their hair and eyes. They, in turn, baptised the Guru. Each man received a new name, **Singh**, which means 'Lion'. Women members were to be called **Kaur**, 'princess'.

As a sign of their vow the Five Beloved were given the 'Five Ks'.

Kesh, uncut hair, is the most important of the 'Five Ks'. After the hair has been touched with amrit, how can it be cut? Sikhs believe that 'The hair of a Sikh is a symbol of his vow to live for the love of God.'

Kanga, comb, goes with the uncut hair, which must be kept clean and healthy, and covered with a turban. 'The complete man, the man who is the image of God...is a man with hair and a turban on his head.' (Sikhs were allowed to fight wearing turbans instead of helmets – and recently they argued that they should be allowed to wear turbans instead of crash helmets on mopeds. This was permitted by law in the United Kingdom in 1976.)

Kirpan, the sword, stands for God's justice and for freedom. It is the sword of a Knight, to be used only in defence of the weak.

Kara is the steel or iron bracelet. One explanation of this is that it shows the part that women have to play. 'Just as the Holy Mother (Guru Gobind Singh's wife) played her part at the first Sikh Baptism, so the bracelet must guide the hand which holds the sword with restraint.' And iron, unlike gold, represents a simple way of living.

Kaccha, undershorts, were meant to be smart and practical in contrast to the loincloth favoured by Hindus. 'A Sikh with his undershorts can go actively to the battlefield, work on any duty, and perform any service in the Temple.'

THE 'FIVE KS' TODAY

Ahead of the model temple, the great kettle drum, introduced by Guru Hargobind, rides on an open trailer. In front of it stand the men who represent the Five Beloved. They are bearded, and stand barefoot, with drawn swords held before them. In front of them are the five standard bearers. Inside the temple is Gian Singh Surjit, the blind musician, ready to play and sing the Hymn of the Gurus which he knows and loves so well.

These men represent the Five Beloved, the first members of the Khalsa

The kettle drum is ready to take part in the procession

Before the procession moves away we say the Sikh United Prayer, the **Ardas**:

'Remember the Five Beloved...
Remember those who remained steadfast in the faith...
Who lived in remembrance of God...
And shared their earnings with others...
Who fed the hungry with food,
and protected the weak with the sword...'

'*Waheguru*' (Wondrous is the Lord!) comes the reply.

Now the great kettle drum sounds, and the procession moves slowly away. Among them are young people, just baptised, who have become new members of the Khalsa this very day.

A YOUNG SIKH EXPLAINS

I asked Raji, a young baptised Sikh herself, to explain what it all meant. Gobind Singh lived nearly 300 years ago. Why should anyone want to join the Brotherhood in twentieth century Britain? Raji explained the meaning of the 'Five Ks' today.

"I was baptised when I was seventeen", said Raji. "I had started to wear the 'Five Ks' when I was fifteen, and I wore them right through College." Raji's kirpan is a small one which hangs from a band. "It's easier for work," she said. Being a baptised Sikh is a strict way of life. "You can't eat meat, drink or smoke. The Sikh scriptures do not forbid the eating of meat, but many baptised Sikhs are vegetarians. You have to pray night and morning, and take a bath." What about the future? Marriage? Raji thought about that then said, "It's much easier to get on if you marry a baptised Sikh."

Raji joined the Khalsa of her own free will. Her parents did not try to force her, but she says that their example did influence her decision. They too are baptised Sikhs.

Raji has never regretted being baptised, although she did rather lose interest for a while. "A lot depends on who you are with. I was more into the pop world at that time, though not totally into discos! I think you should see all sides of life," she told me.

As for the non-baptised Sikhs: "Some are down the pub one day and next day in the gurdwara." Not that it's a sin to be in the pub. "But if you are a baptised Sikh you shouldn't drink."

As for the long daily prayers – twenty to forty minutes – Raji doesn't think they are dull or impossible to keep up. And "There are cassettes which can be played with the prayers. If I feel very down I'll listen to them."

And what about the troubles in India? The death of Bhindranwale? "The attack on the Golden Temple hurt me a lot," Raji said. She has been on several protest marches, condemning the policy of the Indian government. And what about sharing the faith with others? What about those who give it all up?

"If I see them going the wrong way I'll try to bring them back," said Raji. "I wouldn't say, 'get baptised'. That's their choice. But I might say, 'come along with me to the temple.'"

What do you remember?

Join these sentences correctly:

1. AMRIT means   lion
2. SINGH means   wondrous is the Lord
3. KAUR means   nectar
4. WAHEGURU means   princess

What do you know?

Complete these sentences using the correct words:

5. Guru Gobind Singh
   a) wrote the Sikh scriptures.
   b) set up the Khalsa (Sikh Brotherhood).
   c) died in an attack on the Golden Temple.
   d) introduced a big kettledrum into the Sikh religion.
6. The Five Beloved
   a) were the first followers of Nanak.
   b) died for their faith before the Mogul Emperor.
   c) chose the 'Five Ks' to represent the Sikh faith.
   d) were the first to be baptised as Khalsa members.

What do you think?

7. What are the advantages and disadvantages of being a baptised Sikh?
8. The Five Beloved were ready to die for their faith. Would you die for something? Or someone? If so, for what? or for whom?

More things to do

9. Write out and illustrate the words from the prayer Ardas on page 00.
10. Interview someone who is an active member of a religious faith. Find out why they joined and what their faith means for them.

ONE SPIRIT IN TWO BODIES

A Sikh Wedding

The bride arrives at the temple for the wedding ceremony

Navnendar was born in India and came to England as a girl. It seemed a cold sort of place to begin with – the houses were small and you couldn't wear slippers in the garden! She had to work hard at school, to learn English, but her teachers were helpful and she made plenty of friends. The school had a Multi-Racial Youth Council where controversial topics were discussed. What about the Police, for example? Did they understand the Asian community? Did the Asian community really cooperate with the

Navnendar on police duty. She is saying a prayer as the Baisakhi procession passes by

Police? Navnender thought she could help by joining the Police Force herself, and so, after taking her A level exams, she went through Police training and became the first Asian policewoman in her local community.

Martin was one of Navnendar's friends at school. After they left school, he kept in touch with her. Friendship grew into love and they decided to get married. It was a Sikh wedding, with a multi-racial congregation, for Martin and his family are English, while Navnendar's family all come from India.

A Sikh wedding involves three beings – man, woman and God. There is no official priest, for anyone who can read Punjabi may lead a service, but usually there is a recognised Reader, a **Granthi,** to preside. Of course, there must also be skilled musicians for such a joyful occasion! The ceremony should take place before sunrise, but in Britain the time allowed may be extended to twelve noon.

The wedding often takes place in the temple but Navnendar and Martin chose the village hall. First of all, the Scriptures (Guru Granth Sahib) were brought in, an act which turned the hall into a temple for the occasion.

Martin, the bridegroom, was given a place in front of the Scriptures. Navnendar arrived and sat down on his left. The harmonium began to play and the tabla added its rhythm. Hymns were sung, giving good advice to the bride and groom, and explained in English to those guests who did not understand

The bride's father places the groom's scarf in her hands

Punjabi. 'A loaf of dry bread', said one of the songs, 'is full of happiness in the company of the beloved.' Another song declared, 'They are not man and wife who have physical contact only...Only those who have one spirit in two bodies are truly married.'

A Sikh marriage is meant to be for life. There is no divorce.

Now came the heart of the ceremony. The crest was removed from Martin's turban, for bride and groom must walk humbly as they make their vows before God. Then Navnendar's father took the scarf that hung from Martin's shoulder and placed it in his daughter's hand. They then walked four times round the Scriptures, clockwise, while the musicians sang the Wedding Hymn of Guru Ram Das.

The first verse of the Hymn declares that marriage is holy. You do not have to live on your own, like a hermit in the forest, in order to please God. Having children together is also a good way to serve him.

Navnendar and Martin got up again and went slowly round the

The bride and groom circle the Scriptures

Scriptures for the second time. Now the Hymn reminded everyone that God was present. 'By singing his praises,' said the Hymn, 'You behold his very presence...The Lord God is the Soul of the universe.'

In the Third Circle of the ceremony, Navnendar and Martin were reminded that they should remain close to the Sikh community. God is everywhere, but the best place to find him is in company with other people who try to serve Him. 'Good fortune,' says the Hymn, 'has brought me into the company of the Saints. My heart is now absorbed in the name of God.'

The harmonium played on, and the tabla gave a louder, stronger beat. Once more around the Guru Granth Sahib and the knot of love would be tied. Martin was in for a surprise! No one had mentioned that family and friends would throw flower petals over bride and groom during the fourth and last Circle! Everyone stood up as the final verse of the Wedding Hymn declared one of the great beliefs of the Sikh faith: in marriage, man and woman should be truly united, and in the end the Soul should be truly united with God as well.

'In the Fourth Circle, knowledge of God becomes complete in the mind, and union with Him becomes complete. Nanak says: "In the fourth round you have become one with the Lord."' (All the hymns of the Granth are credited to Guru Nanak as the inspiration for them, even when they have been composed by other people.)

Navnendar and Martin were now married. The Reader opened the Scriptures at random and chose a special text, a Vak, just for them. It said: 'You have chosen to be married and God has helped you, so devote more time to thinking about Him.'

After this, everyone stood up, while the priest said the united Prayer of the Sikhs, the Ardas:

'Lord, give to the Sikhs,
the gift of charity,
the gift of the sanctity of hair,
the gift of disciplined life
the gift of tolerance and trust,
the gift of all gifts – the Divine Name.'

"Wonderful Lord!" was the reply of the people.

Next there was something sweet to eat for everybody – a helping of **karah parshad**, the warm and tasty pudding which you eat with your fingers. Eating karah parshad brings everyone together in friendship and faith.

And after that, photographs, more food and drink, and dancing...It was a very happy day.

A fortnight after their wedding, Navnendar and Martin went along to the temple to a thanksgiving ceremony. Martin was given a prayer book, a **gutka**, and a small cloth, a **romalla**, to cover it. This was a way of saying, "welcome to the Sikh community." At the end of the service, the Scriptures were again opened at random to find a message from God to the newly married pair. Strangely, it was the very same text that had been given at the wedding!

'You have chosen to be married and God has helped you, so devote more time to thinking about Him.'

What do you remember?

Join these sentences correctly:

1. A VAK is · · · · · · · a prayer book.
2. A ROMALLA is · · · · · a sweet pudding.
3. A GUTKA is · · · · · · words from the Scriptures
   chosen at random.
4. KARAH PARSHAD is · · · a cloth to cover the
   prayer book.

What do you know?

Complete these sentences using the correct words:

5. In a Sikh wedding, the bride
   and groom must:

   a) sing the wedding hymn of
   Ram Das.
   b) walk four times round the
   Scriptures.
   c) wait untill after 12 noon.
   d) belong to the same caste.

What do you think?

6. Do you agree that getting married can bring people closer to God?
7. 'Only those who have one spirit in two bodies are truly married.' Do you
   agree with this?
8. 'Marriage is meant to be for life.' Is divorce too easy nowadays? Or not
   easy enough?

More things to do

9. Make a poem-poster using these words from the Marriage Hymn:

   'Through the Guru's instruction
   the union is made easy,
   and the sweetness of my beloved
   fills my body and soul.
   God has completed this marriage,
   and the bride's heart rejoices in his name.'

10. Find out what you can about the marriage customs of other religions
    and see whether they express similar or different ideas.

THIS IS MY FRIEND
WHO RODE ON MY BACK

Puran Singh Founds a Pingalwara

*I*n the city of Lahore, now part of Pakistan, there stands a great Sikh temple (called Dera Sahib). It is built on the spot where Arjan, the fourth Guru, was tortured to death on the orders of the emperor Jehangir in 1606 CE. Every year a great memorial service is held there, as worshippers gather to sing the brave Arjan's own hymns.

'Remember your God', these words of his are inscribed on the shrine, 'and your bodies shall be free from disease.' The hymn goes on, 'I have uttered...the hymns of God. O my brothers always sing, listen and read them.'

Arjan died a martyr. It is said that his body blended with the light and could not be found anywhere.

In the year 1934, an unwanted baby was left on the road outside the temple. He could not cry, for he was deaf and dumb, and his body was disabled. His parents had left him at the temple to die. What else could they do?

But a young man named Puran Singh came along and picked the baby up.

PURAN SINGH

Puran Singh was born into a Hindu family in 1905. He wanted to learn, but had to drop out of school because there was no money to

Bhagat Puran Singh

pay the fees. The teaching of the Sikh Gurus attracted him greatly, and he spent much of his time praying and **meditating** at the Dera Sahib Temple in Lahore. Puran Singh also loved the Shahid Ganj Temple, which commemorates Mani Singh, a scribe who wrote down the entire Scriptures when the tenth Guru recited them from memory! Mani also refused to pay a heavy tax imposed by the Muslim Governor in exchange for permission to hold the festival of **Divali**. And so, in 1738, he too was executed.

Young Puran Singh thought a great deal about the martyrs, who had been ready to give up their lives for God. He decided to do the same: but for him this was to mean long life, not early death. He took a vow of celibacy (to have no sexual relationships) and he devoted his life to prayer.

Although Puran Singh had been forced to leave school early, he did as much reading as he could. Sikhs believe that God speaks through other religions, and Puran Singh became an admirer of William Booth, a Christian who founded The Salvation Army, 'to love the unlovable and befriend the friendless'. When Puran found the abandoned baby outside the temple in Lahore, it seemed to him like a challenge from God. He picked the baby up.

For fourteen years he carried the **pingal**, as a disabled child is called. He became a familiar sight on the streets of Lahore, as he tried to practise the teaching of Guru Nanak:

'To whom shall I offer flowers in worship?
At whose feet shall I fall?
I call myself a slave of all your slaves, O Lord.
There is no other way to meet the Lord of the whole World.'

Bhagat Puran Singh rides with the 'pingal' in the cart belonging to the Refuge. The Punjabi words mean Amritsar Pingalwara

People gave Puran Singh the title **Bhagat**, which means 'devotee' – 'one who believes in God.'

Narain Singh, an Indian writer, recalls those days: "I first met Bhagat Ji" ('Ji' is added to someone's name as a mark of respect), he writes, "about the year 1940, when he walked barefoot and half naked on the streets of Lahore, usually with a crippled boy as his sacred load on his back, picking up things like pieces of stone and metal, banana peel, nails, horseshoes and brickbats that might interfere with the convenience and safety of vehicles and the public."

The pingal grew bigger and heavier. Few knew that the child was a foundling: and some who did were only too ready to laugh. You might carry your own child, but why on earth bother with an unknown? "With our people," writes Narain Singh, "the spectacle of a helpless patient dying on the roadside is taken as the inevitable fate of a human being."

Puran Singh planned to change that. And not everyone made fun of him. Diwan Anand Kumar, formerly Vice-Chancellor of Punjab University, recalls his work. "I vividly remember him walking from the Temple of Guru Arjan to my office in the University laboratory, for miles, frequently, on errands of goodwill for the help and relief of students and people in distress. I am very proud of being a friend of such a noble soul."

Puran Singh has tried to live out the Sikh faith in twentieth century style. He has tried to be both a Bhagat, a lover of God, and a Servant of the People at the same time. In Indian thinking there are three ways to find truth – Love, Knowledge and Action. 'All three,' writes Narain Singh, 'should go hand in hand, or human personality would be incomplete. If you want to help someone who is ill, for example, you must also take Action guided by Love. If a man serves a sick person without possessing sympathy, then according to Narain Singh, 'it becomes a monotony for him and a burden for him who is served.'

Puran Singh has always tried to show Love for God by taking Action on behalf of helpless people. 'It was the love of mankind,' writes Narain Singh, 'that carried him to the love of God...The service of God has remained for him the love, the worship and the service of the people.'

THE PARTITION OF INDIA

The love of humankind was in short supply in 1947, when India was divided and refugees fled eastwards and westwards, carrying what they could of their belongings, and leaving land, houses and jobs behind. Lahore was included in Pakistan and Puran Singh had to flee, along with other Sikhs. He carried with him his pingal, now a fully grown and heavy young man.

But a year later, now in Amritsar, the holiest city of the Sikhs, Puran Singh founded the first **Pingalwara** or Refuge for disabled people. From this small beginning has grown the All-India Pingalwara Society.

'The Pingalwara,' writes Anand Kumar, 'has existed in his (Puran Singh's) dreams from his early youth...the act of carrying about the disabled boy on his back is symbolic of his carrying the whole institution – housing the aged, the infirm, the disabled and the sick on his shoulders.'

In 1988 Puran Singh was visited by Derek Brown of the London *Guardian* newspaper. Derek Brown found that the work of caring for disabled people had gone on in spite of unrest in the city, including the battle for the GoldenTemple. Puran Singh still tramps the streets of the city, begging money to feed his growing army of destitute people. There are about 300 of them now, housed in four centres.

You might be disturbed by conditions in the Pingalwara. In the home for mentally ill or disabled women (see photo), rats scuttle round the rubble in the courtyard. On three sides there are open wards, where the women lie blank-eyed or muttering. In the children's ward, boys squat in line in a concrete yard, patiently waiting for their meal of lentils and bread.

But in a city whose only State mental hospital has a waiting list of five years, a Pingalwara is more than home. It is the difference between life – and death on the streets.

In Sikh temples in Britain you may find a collecting box in aid of the work begun by Puran Singh. 'The Pingalwara,' writes Narain Singh, 'is a Temple of God without any idol. The only symbol of God in the Pingalwara is the destitute, bodily helpless, man.'

A pingalwara in Amritsar

And in the main Refuge in Amritsar you can still find the first pingal who was left outside the temple in Lahore. He is hunched and twisted in his chair and he cannot speak, but "Look here," says Puran Singh; "This is my friend who rode on my back for all those years. He is how it all began."

What do you remember?

Join these sentences correctly:

1. A PINGAL is   an Indian festival.
2. DEHRA SAHIB is   a disabled person.
3. A PINGALWARA is   a temple.
4. DIVALI is   a shelter for homeless and afflicted people.

What do you know?

5. Complete these sentences using the correct words:

The turning point in Puran Singh's life was when:

a) he had to leave school.

b) he picked up an abandoned child.

c) India was divided in 1947.

d) he was visited by Derek Brown.

What do you think?

6. Puran Singh took a vow of celibacy (to stay unmarried). What are the advantages and disadvantages of living in this way?
7. Nowadays some people can choose to terminate a pregnancy rather than have a severely disabled child like the pingal. Is this progress? Or a step backwards?

More things to do

8. Try to imagine the thoughts of the man or woman who left the pingal at the temple. Make up a prayer which they might have said.
9. In Indian thinking, Knowledge, Love and Action are paths to truth. Write a play in which three people try to help someone:

   A has love but not enough knowledge.

   B has knowledge but doesn't like to take action.

   C is keen to act but not very loving.
10. Look at the pictures of Bhagat Puran Singh, and write a story beginning:

    "Here comes that crazy fellow – still got a dumb chap on his back...."

    "Maybe it's his brother."

    "He picked him out of the gutter! Let's have some fun with them..."

More Than I Asked For

The Healing of Baldav Singh

*I*n June 1987 young Baldav Singh was riding his bike in Yarnton Road, Thamesmead, London. Along came a speeding car. It hit Baldav, injuring him seriously.

An ambulance took him to the nearby Brook Hospital. Hearing the terrible news, Baldav's mother, Mrs Jastinder Kaur Sahemi, rushed round to the hospital. Things were worse than she feared!

"I couldn't see him when I arrived at the hospital because his injuries were so bad," said Mrs Sahemi. "It was quite some time before I could go to him. He was in the intensive care department. The doctors explained the situation and gave me no hope at all. They said even if he came through he would be a vegetable. I had nothing left but to pray, which I did, holding his hand all the time in the intensive care ward." And she was not the only person to pray. Baldav's grandmother, who is an expert in the Sikh Scriptures, was praying too.

Jastinder, Baldav's mother, at prayer

Mrs Sahemi came to England from India at the age of ten. She prayed in Punjabi, using the first three prayers of the **Japji** – the Sikh morning prayer.

'Who can sing God, who forms the body and then reduces it to dust?
Who can sing God, who takes away life and again infuses it?
Who can sing God, who seeks to be far away?
Who can sing God, who sees all, just face to face?'

Unlike Baldav's grandmother, Jastinder cannot read the Scriptures for herself. "All I knew I said," she declares. "I prayed to God and I asked for Baldav's life. Even if I didn't know what to ask, all I had to say was 'Sat Nam' – 'His name is true.'

This is a very short and very special prayer. The words, Sat Nam, sum up all the teachings of the Sikh Gurus. If you say the words and mean the prayer, then you are trusting your whole self to God. And Jastinder was asking for nothing for herself. She only wanted Baldav to live!

'Those who taste the sweetness of God's name,' wrote Guru Amar Sad, 'become free from fear'.

And more quickly than she had dared to hope, Jastinder's fears were lifted. Her son began to mend. Baldav was out of hospital after just a week. He could not go back to school for the rest of the summer term, but he was able to start again in the September. He made a complete recovery.

What could his mother do to say 'thank you' to God? She agreed with Baldav's grandmother to hold a special thanksgiving ceremony. The **Akand Path** is a non-stop reading of the Sikh Scriptures. It takes 48 hours to complete and is often held in the temple at festival times. It might be held, for instance, to mark the birthday of Guru Nanak. But you can also hold an Akand Path at home.

And so the great day came at 13 Wolvercot Road. It was the day after Baldav's fourteenth birthday, and a year after the accident. "I was grateful for that year," says Jastinder, "and for many more to come."

During the ceremony hymns are sung. Baldav's grandmother sits behind the Guru Granth Sahib. His mother, Jastinder, is on the right of the picture

Visitors came from as far away as Birmingham. The Holy Book (Guru Granth Sahib) was brought solemnly from the temple and placed in the front room. The house had now become a temple. And then the ceremony began, each reader taking turns in shifts of two hours.

When an Akand Path takes place, people can come and go during the readings, as long as they show respect to God and the Holy Book. But Baldav was there all the time. He went to bed in front of the Scriptures in the living room.

"I did my best to stay awake," he says, "I thought about the accident. If it wasn't for God I wouldn't be here. Mainly I was just thinking about it. And glad about it."

Baldav's younger brother Jaspal went to bed at half past nine – but he enjoyed the food and the singing (kirtan) that came at the end. Singing the hymns of the Gurus brings the Sikhs closer to each other

Baldav's grandmother gives a blessing during the ceremony.
His mother and younger brother watch

and to God.

Baldav's elder sister, Saran Kaur, was busy in the kitchen for
much of the time. Among other treats for the great day was the
special food (karah parshad). This is made from plain flour cooked
with sugar and clarified butter. Hymns are sung as it is prepared,
and then it is placed on a small stool close to the Scriptures. Karah
parshad is sweet and rather sticky, and when you share it you are
saying that people can all be friends before God.

Baldav's grandmother also wished to give thanks. She gave a
romalla – a special cloth to cover the Guru Granth Sahib. The cloth is

embroidered with five rays, one for each of the Five Beloved who were the founder-members of the Khalsa – the Sikh Brotherhood. She also presented five turbans, to be given to five Sikhs. Baldav also wore a turban for the first time. "It's something to live up to," he says. (This is not the same as joining the Khalsa. Many people who wear turbans are not Khalsa members.)

But what about the driver of the car? "At first I was angry," said Jastinder, "I could have killed him. But then all my feelings were for Baldav. As he got better my bitterness went. At the court the driver couldn't remember what happened. He was going too fast – but he did stop. I don't hold a grudge. I don't hate."

"Even though it's not out loud," said Jastinder, "I say thanks to God every day of my life. He gave what I asked for – and more."

Baldav's mother, Jastinder, carries the Guru Granth Sahib from her home on its journey back to the temple

What do you remember?

Join these sentences correctly:

1. AKAND PATH is   the Sikh morning prayer.
2. JAPJI is   a 48-hour read of
   theScriptures.
3. KIRTAN is   a prayer, 'His name is true'.
4. SAT NAM is   hymn singing.

What do you know?

5. Complete this sentence correctly:

   God gave Jastinder more than
   she asked because:

   a) Baldav survived.
   b) Baldav made a complete
      recovery.
   c) the driver who struck him
      was caught.
   d) she was able to forgive the
      driver.

What do you think?

6. Was Jastinder's prayer really answered? Or was it wishful thinking?
   How could you decide?
7. Can people be healed through medical treatment *and* prayer? Does it
   have to be one or the other? Does it depend on the type of illness?

More things to do

8. Find out what followers of other religions do in order to seek healing.
9. Look in the newspapers for reports of other healings which are thought
   to be in answer to prayer. Make a scrapbook or display of them.

WORD LIST

Akal Takht	'The Eternal Throne', built in Amritsar by Guru Hargobind
Akand Path	A non-stop reading of the Scriptures
Amrit	Nectar: a mixture of water and sugar used in baptism
Amrit Kirtan	Popular hymns found in the Sikh Holy Book, the Granth
Ardas	A united prayer of the Sikhs
Asceticism	A very strict way of life, chosen by someone who sees it as a means of getting closer to God
Baisakhi	The Sikh New Year Festival
Bhagat	A devotee – someone totally givento God
Caste	The system of groups into which Hindus were born. There were four groups: Priests, Warriors,Traders and Farmers. Below these came the 'Untouchables'
Divali	The Festival of Light
Granth	The Sikh Scriptures. Also called the Adi Granth and the Guru Granth Sahib
Granthi	Reader of the sacred texts
Gurdwara	A Sikh temple. It means 'the Guru's door'. Also spelt gurudwara
Gurmukhi	The script used to write Punjabi. Also the old Punjabi language of the Scriptures
Guru	'Teacher': It may refer to 1) God 2) the Ten (human) Gurus 3) the Sikh Scriptures
Gutka	Prayer book
Harijan	'Children of God': a name now given to the people outside the caste system formerly known as 'Untouchables'
Harimandir	The Golden Temple in Amritsar
Hukam	The will of God: when you choose a place in the Scriptures at random
Ik oankar	'God is One'
Islam	The religion of followers of the prophet Muhammad
Japji	The morning prayer

Kaccha	Undershorts: one of the 'Five Ks'
Kanga	A comb: one of the 'Five Ks'
Kara	A steel bracelet: one of the 'Five Ks'
Karah parshad	Special food, offered to God and then shared
Kaur	'Princess': name given to a woman who has joined the Khalsa
Kesh	Hair: never to be cut by a faithful Sikh
Khanda	The Sikh emblem
Khalsa	The Sikh Brotherhood – men and women who make a special promise to serve Godand who are baptised. It means 'the pure'
Kirpan	Sword: one of the 'Five Ks'
Kirtan	Singing together at a service or ceremony
Langar	The common dining hall in a temple
Lavan	The wedding hymn. It means 'circling' because bride and groom go round the Scriptures four times
Maya	Illusion: the world of selfishness that keeps people from God
Meditation	A way of concentrating on what your mind is saying to you, thinking calmly and quietly
Monotheism	Belief in One God
Mool Mantra	'Root belief': verses that sum up the Sikh faith
Mukti	Deliverance: escaping from Maya and the cycle of rebirth, and becoming one with God
Nam	The Name of God
Nishan sahib	The flag of the Sikhs
Partition	The dividing of the land into India and Pakistan in 1947
Polytheism	Belief in many gods
Pingal	A Refuge for disabled people
Reincarnation	The belief that a person may be 'reborn' many times. After death, the soul may return to live in another body
Romalla	A cover specially made for the Scriptures
Sangat	The Sikh Community
Sati	Suicide of widows after the death of their husbands
Sat Nam	'True Name', God's name is true
Singh	'Lion': name given to a man who joins the Khalsa
Tabla	A pair of drums played with the hands
Vak	A special text, chosen at random out of the Holy Book, to guide a person's thinking